ON THE FARM

First published in the UK in 1998 by
Belitha Press Limited, London House, Great Eastern Wharf,
Parkgate Road, London SW11 4NQ

This paperback edition first published in 1999

Series devised by Philip Ardagh

Philip Ardagh asserts his moral right to be
identified as the author of this work.

ISBN 1 85561 855 9 (paperback)
ISBN 1 85561 803 6 (hardback)

British Library Cataloguing in Publication Data for this
book is available from the British Library

Printed in China

Editor: Honor Head
Designer: Simeen Karim
Illustrator: Tig Sutton

ON THE FARM

By Philip Ardagh
Illustrated by Tig Sutton

 Belitha Press

It's always busy on the farm.

Here comes a combine harvester to cut the wheat.

The stalks of wheat come out of the back. The grains of wheat are kept inside.

Here comes a tractor and
trailer to collect the grain.

The tractor drives beside
the combine harvester.
Grain is poured
into the trailer.

Here comes a tractor and
baler to pick up the stalks.

The stalks are scooped into the baler and come out as bales of straw.

Here comes a tractor with
a bale fork on the front.

The fork spikes a bale
and lifts it up in the air.

Here comes a truck to collect the bales.

The bales are put on the back of the truck which takes them to the barn to be stored.

Here comes a plough
to plough up the field.

The plough cuts into the soil
to make it ready for planting.

Here comes a tractor and seed drill
to plant next year's crops.

The seed drill makes holes in the soil. Then it drops seeds into the holes and covers them over.

Here comes a huge tanker
to collect the milk.

The milk from the cows is stored
inside the tanker.

Here comes a horsebox to collect the farmer's pony.

The pony walks up the
ramp into the horsebox.

The farmer and his family
are off to the horse show.

But first they must wait for the ducks to cross the lane.